BARBRA
Love is the answer

Photography by Firooz Zahedi, www.firoozzahedi.com

Piano/vocal arrangements by John Nicholas

Cherry Lane Music Company
Director of Publications/Project Editor: Mark Phillips
Publications Coordinator: Rebecca Skidmore

ISBN: 978-1-60378-214-2

Visit our website at www.cherrylaneprint.com

it happened in monterey...

not so very long ago, Barbra attended my performance at the jazz festival. The next time we met, at a party, we fell to talking about songs that she might feature on her upcoming tour.

In 2006 I attended her sold-out concert at Madison Square Garden. We got to talking about songs again during the after-party in her hotel suite. From these exchanges sprang the idea of entering the studio together, only I would be sitting on the more unusual side of the glass.

So, how do you start to work on a record such as this? A shot in the dark, a chance remark, a list of songs in the mail. Short notes and conversations, a few cocktails and some laughter. These are the steps you take.

What do you bring to a woman who has already made so many brilliant records and is so accomplished in everything she does?

Now, we are all sharing the charged and precious space of Capital Studios, in which our singer daily illustrates that her famous appetite for high style and the drama of life also extends to curiously about songs that are still to be sung.

There is nothing coy or flimsy about her approach to love as a musical subject. She is a woman in her finest hour, looking back with some melancholy and humility at the comedy of life. She hunts down that crucial vocal nuance which exults and laments in equal measure.

When I first heard Barbra's records, her voice and style were simply mesmerizing. They still are. The thought of meeting her incredibly high standards was a bit daunting.

This has been an extraordinary project to be a part of. From the opening celebratory statement of "Here's to Life" to the unadorned beauty of the solo piano–accompanied "You Must Believe in Spring," she is unflinching and utterly uncompromising.

Finally, during those brief interludes in which technical mysteries must be solved, we play a few hands of gin rummy on a small table in the control room, just two women, sharing a joke and waiting to go back to work.

diana krall

CONTENTS

Here's to Life

Lyrics by
Phyllis Molinary

Music by
Artie Butler

8

In the Wee Small Hours
of the Morning

Words by
Bob Hilliard

Music by
David Mann

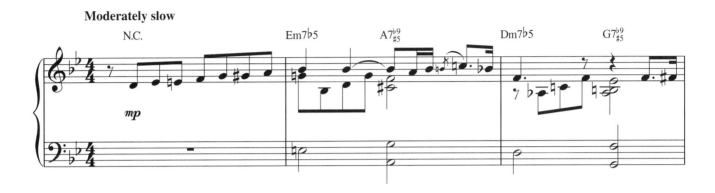

When the sun is high in the

af - ter - noon — sky, you can al - ways find some-thing to do. But from

morn - ing, _____ that's the time you miss him most of all.

When your lone-ly heart _____ has learned its les-son, _____ you'd be his if on-ly he would

Gentle Rain
from the Motion Picture THE GENTLE RAIN

Words by
Matt Dubey

Music by
Luiz Bonfa

If You Go Away

(Ne me quitte pas)

English Words by
Rod McKuen

French Words and Music by
Jacques Brel

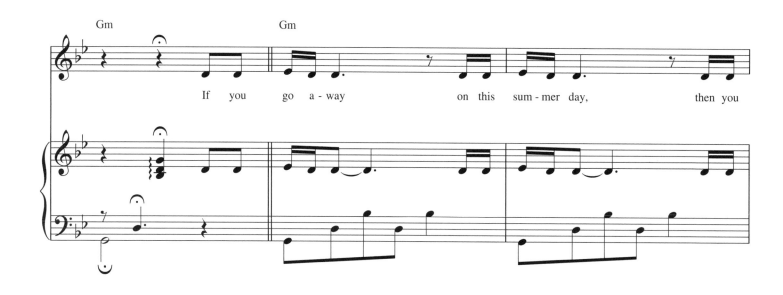

If you go a-way on this sum-mer day, then you

might as well take the sun a-way. All the birds that flew in the

Spring Can Really
Hang You Up the Most

Lyric by
Fran Landesman

Music by
Tommy Wolf

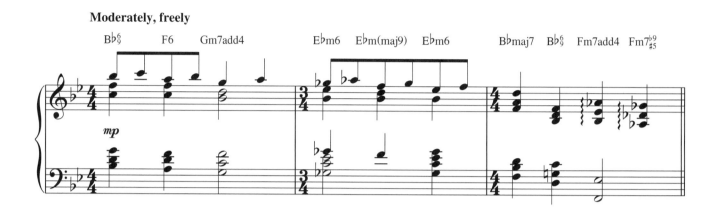

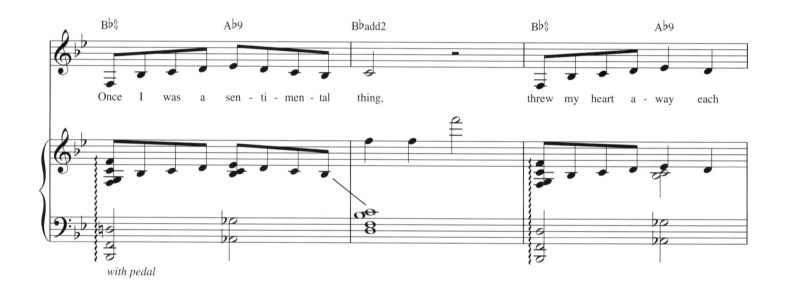

Love came my way, hoped __ it would last. _____

We had our day; _____ now that's all _____ in the past.

Spring came a - long, a sea - son of song,

full of sweet prom - ise, _____ but some - thing went wrong.

Make Someone Happy
from DO RE MI

Words by
Betty Comden and Adolph Green

Music by
Jule Styne

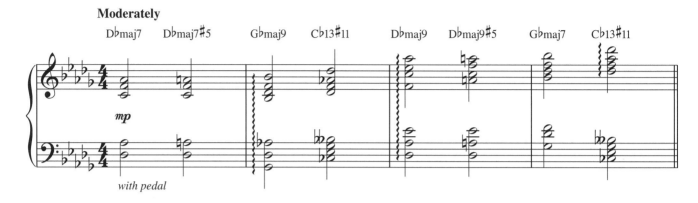

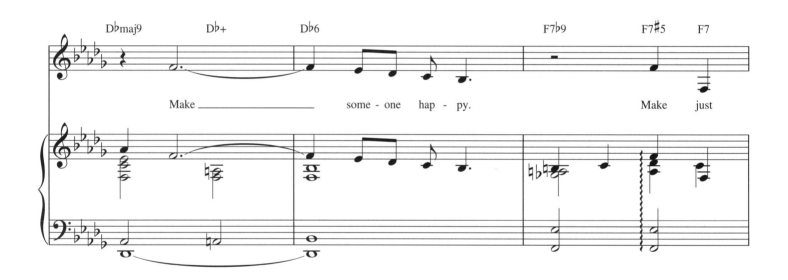

Make _____ some-one hap-py. Make just

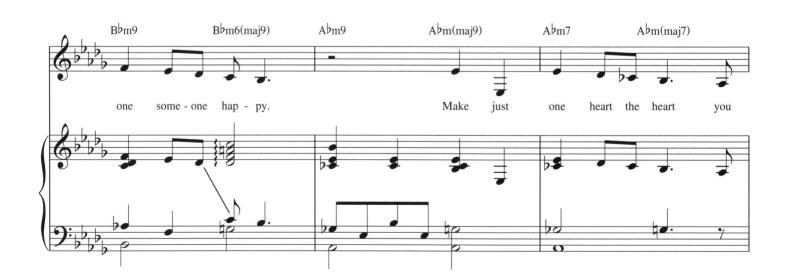

one some-one hap-py. Make just one heart the heart you

Where Do You Start?

Lyric by
Alan and Marilyn Bergman

Music by
Johnny Mandel

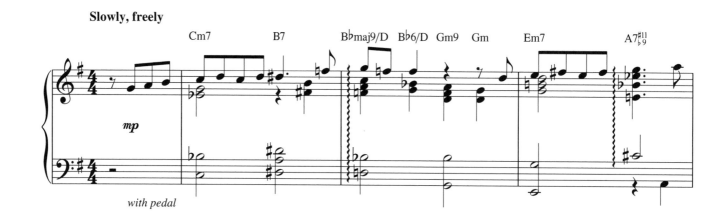

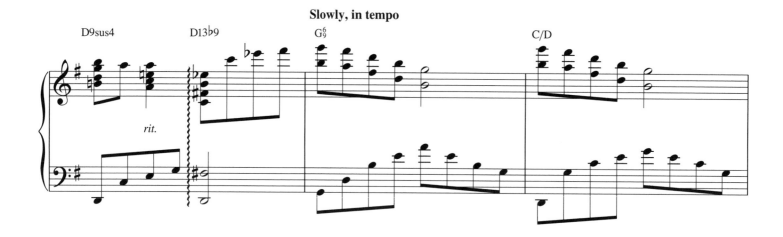

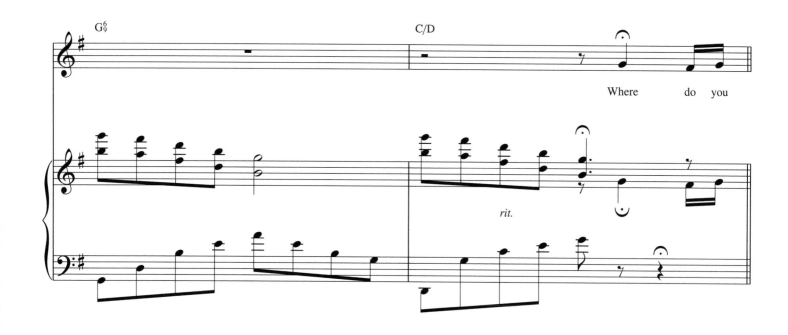

Where do you

Slowly, with a beat

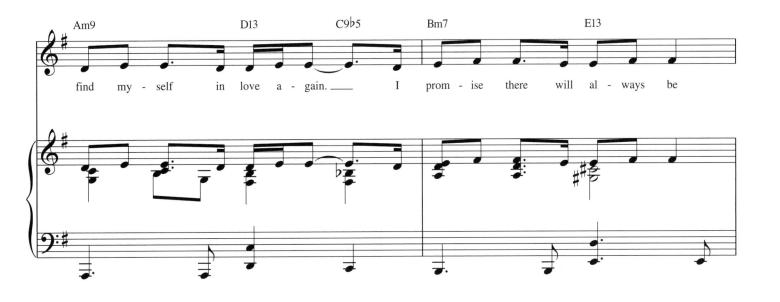

find my-self in love a-gain.___ I prom - ise there will al - ways be

a lit - tle place no one will see, a ti - ny part deep in my heart that

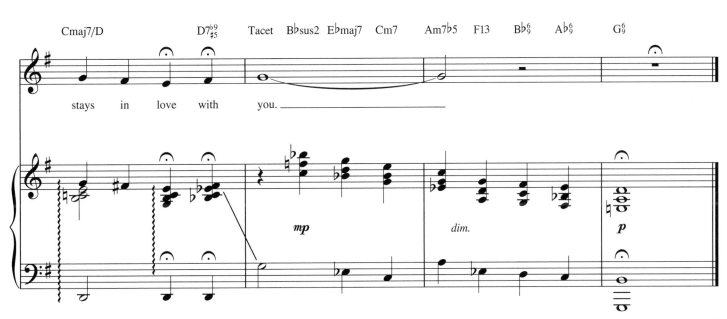

stays in love with you.___

A Time for Love
from AN AMERICAN DREAM

Words by
Paul Francis Webster

Music by
Johnny Mandel

time _____ for sum - mer skies, _____ for hum - ming - birds and

As _____

time goes drift-ing by, the wil-low _____ bends _____ and

52

so do I. _____ But oh, my friends, what - ev - er sky a -

Freely, slowly

bove, _____ I've known a time for spring, a

time for fall, but best of all, a time for

love. _____

Here's That Rainy Day

Words by
Johnny Burke

Music by
Jimmy Van Heusen

Love Dance

Words and Music by
Paul H. Williams, Ivan Guimaraes Lins
and Gilson Peranzetta

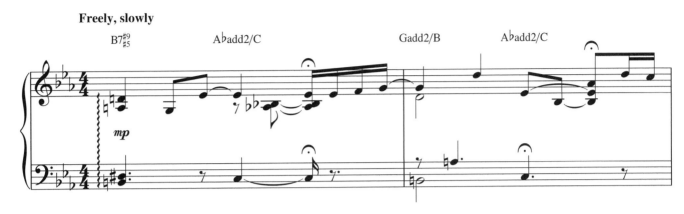

From too much talk to si-lent touch-es, sweet __ touch-es. __

61

Smoke Gets in Your Eyes

from ROBERTA

Words by
Otto Harbach

Music by
Jerome Kern

Some Other Time

from ON THE TOWN

Lyrics by
Betty Comden and Adolph Green

Music by
Leonard Bernstein

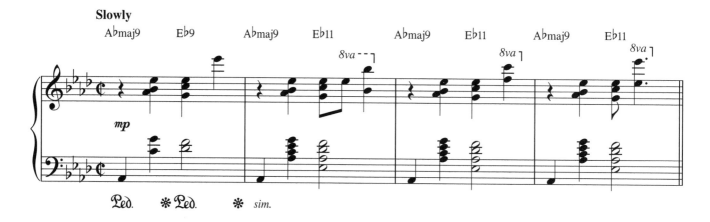

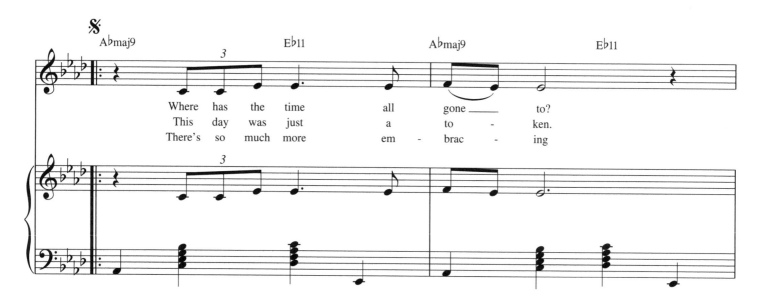

Where has the time all gone to?
This day was just a to - ken.
There's so much more em - brac - ing

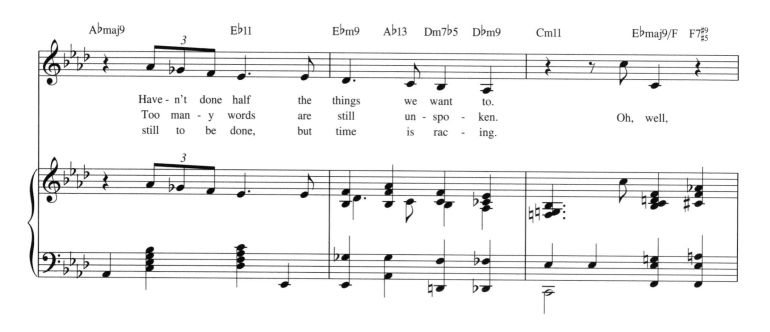

Have - n't done half the things we want to.
Too man - y words are still un - spo - ken.
still to be done, but time is rac - ing.

Oh, well,

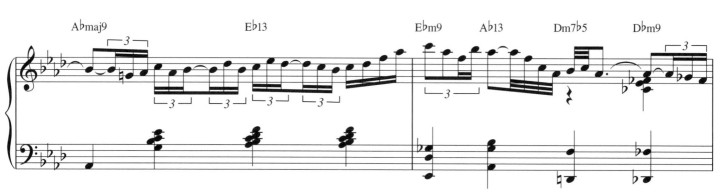

You Must Believe in Spring

Lyrics by
Alan and Marilyn Bergman

Music by
Michel Legrand

great songs series

This legendary series has delighted players and performers for generations.

Great Songs of Country Music

This volume features 58 country gems, including: Abilene • Afternoon Delight • Amazed • Annie's Song • Blue • Crazy • Elvira • Fly Away • For the Good Times • Friends in Low Places • The Gambler • Hey, Good Lookin' • I Hope You Dance • Thank God I'm a Country Boy • This Kiss • Your Cheatin' Heart • and more.
02500503 P/V/G..................................$19.95

Great Songs of Folk Music

Nearly 50 of the most popular folk songs of our time, including: Blowin' in the Wind • The House of the Rising Sun • Puff the Magic Dragon • This Land Is Your Land • Time in a Bottle • The Times They Are A-Changin' • The Unicorn • Where Have All the Flowers Gone? • and more.
02500997 P/V/G..................................$19.95

Great Songs from The Great American Songbook

52 American classics, including: Ain't That a Kick in the Head • As Time Goes By • Come Fly with Me •Georgia on My Mind • I Get a Kick Out of You • I've Got You Under My Skin • The Lady Is a Tramp • Love and Marriage • Mack the Knife • Misty • Over the Rainbow • People • Take the "A" Train • Thanks for the Memory • and more.
02500760 P/V/G..................................$16.95

Great Songs of the Fifties

Features rock, pop, country, Broadway and movie tunes, including: All Shook Up • At the Hop • Blue Suede Shoes • Dream Lover • Fly Me to the Moon • Kansas City • Love Me Tender • Misty • Peggy Sue • Rock Around the Clock • Sea of Love • Sixteen Tons • Take the "A" Train • Wonderful! Wonderful! • and more. Includes an introduction by award-winning journalist Bruce Pollock.
02500323 P/V/G..................................$16.95

Great Songs of the Sixties, Vol. 1 – Revised

The updated version of this classic book includes 80 faves from the 1960s: Angel of the Morning • Bridge over Troubled Water • Cabaret • Different Drum • Do You Believe in Magic • Eve of Destruction • Monday, Monday • Spinning Wheel • Walk on By • and more.
02509902 P/V/G..................................$19.95

Great Songs of the Sixties, Vol. 2 – Revised

61 more '60s hits: California Dreamin' • Crying • For Once in My Life • Honey • Little Green Apples • MacArthur Park • Me and Bobby McGee • Nowhere Man • Piece of My Heart • Sugar, Sugar • You Made Me So Very Happy • and more.
02509904 P/V/G..................................$19.95

Great Songs of the Seventies, Vol. 1 – Revised

This super collection of 70 big hits from the '70s includes: After the Love Has Gone • Afternoon Delight • Annie's Song • Band on the Run • Cold as Ice • FM • Imagine • It's Too Late • Layla • Let It Be • Maggie May • Piano Man • Shelter from the Storm • Superstar • Sweet Baby James • Time in a Bottle • The Way We Were • and more.
02509917 P/V/G..................................$19.95

Great Songs of the Eighties – Revised

This edition features 50 songs in rock, pop & country styles, plus hits from Broadway and the movies! Songs: Almost Paradise • Angel of the Morning • Do You Really Want to Hurt Me • Endless Love • Flashdance...What a Feeling • Guilty • Hungry Eyes • (Just Like) Starting Over • Let Love Rule • Missing You • Patience • Through the Years • Time After Time • Total Eclipse of the Heart • and more.
02502125 P/V/G..................................$18.95

Great Songs of the Nineties

Includes: Achy Breaky Heart • Beautiful in My Eyes • Believe • Black Hole Sun • Black Velvet • Blaze of Glory • Building a Mystery • Crash into Me • Fields of Gold • From a Distance • Glycerine • Here and Now • Hold My Hand • I'll Make Love to You • Ironic • Linger • My Heart Will Go On • Waterfalls • Wonderwall • and more.
02500040 P/V/G..................................$16.95

Great Songs of Broadway

This fabulous collection of 60 standards includes: Getting to Know You • Hello, Dolly! • The Impossible Dream • Let Me Entertain You • My Favorite Things • My Husband Makes Movies • Oh, What a Beautiful Mornin' • On My Own • People • Tomorrow • Try to Remember • Unusual Way • What I Did for Love • and dozens more, plus an introductory article.
02500615 P/V/G..................................$19.95

Great Songs for Children

90 wonderful, singable favorites kids love: Baa Baa Black Sheep • Bingo • The Candy Man • Do-Re-Mi • Eensy Weensy Spider • The Hokey Pokey • Linus and Lucy • Sing • This Old Man • Yellow Submarine • and more, with a touching foreword by Grammy-winning singer/songwriter Tom Chapin.
02501348 P/V/G..................................$19.99

Great Songs of Classic Rock

Nearly 50 of the greatest songs of the rock era, including: Against the Wind • Cold As Ice • Don't Stop Believin' • Feels like the First Time • I Can See for Miles • Maybe I'm Amazed • Minute by Minute • Money • Nights in White Satin • Only the Lonely • Open Arms • Rikki Don't Lose That Number • Rosanna • We Are the Champions • and more.
02500801 P/V/G..................................$19.95

Great Songs of the Movies

Nearly 60 of the best songs popularized in the movies, including: Accidentally in Love • Alfie • Almost Paradise • The Rainbow Connection • Somewhere in My Memory • Take My Breath Away (Love Theme) • Three Coins in the Fountain • (I've Had) the Time of My Life • Up Where We Belong • The Way We Were • and more.
02500967 P/V/G..................................$19.95

Great Songs of the Pop Era

Over 50 hits from the pop era, including: Every Breath You Take • I'm Every Woman • Just the Two of Us • Leaving on a Jet Plane • My Cherie Amour • Raindrops Keep Fallin' on My Head • Time After Time • (I've Had) the Time of My Life • What a Wonderful World • and more.
02500043 Easy Piano..........................$16.95

Great Songs of 2000-2009

Over 50 of the decade's biggest hits, including: Accidentally in Love • Breathe (2 AM) • Daughters • Hanging by a Moment • The Middle • The Remedy (I Won't Worry) • Smooth • A Thousand Miles • and more.
02500922 P/V/G..................................$24.99

Great Songs for Weddings

A beautiful collection of 59 pop standards perfect for wedding ceremonies and receptions, including: Always and Forever • Amazed • Beautiful in My Eyes • Can You Feel the Love Tonight • Endless Love • Love of a Lifetime • Open Arms • Unforgettable • When I Fall in Love • The Wind Beneath My Wings • and more.
02501006 P/V/G..................................$19.95

Prices, contents, and availability subject to change without notice.

www.cherrylane.com

7777 W. Bluemound Rd. P.O. Box 13819 Milwaukee, WI 53213

0610

More Great Piano/Vocal Books

FROM CHERRY LANE

For a complete listing of Cherry Lane titles available,
including contents listings, please visit our web site at
www.cherrylane.com

02501136 Sara Bareilles – Little Voice . . .$16.95	02503701 Man of La Mancha $11.95	02500515 Barbra Streisand –
02502171 The Best of Boston $17.95	02501047 Dave Matthews Band –	Christmas Memories $16.95
02501123 Buffy the Vampire Slayer –	Anthology $24.95	02507969 Barbra Streisand – A Collection:
Once More with Feeling $18.95	02500693 Dave Matthews – Some Devil . . .$16.95	Greatest Hits and More $17.95
02500665 Sammy Cahn Songbook $24.95	02500493 Dave Matthews Band – Live in Chicago	02502164 Barbra Streisand – The Concert .$22.95
02501454 Colbie Caillat – Breakthrough . .$17.99	12/19/98 at the United Center .$14.95	02500550 Essential Barbra Streisand $24.95
02501127 Colbie Caillat – Coco $16.95	02502192 Dave Matthews Band –	02502228 Barbra Streisand –
02500144 Mary Chapin Carpenter –	Under the Table and Dreaming .$17.95	Higher Ground $16.95
Party Doll & Other Favorites . . .$16.95	02501504 John Mayer – Battle Studies . . .$19.99	02501065 Barbra Streisand –
02502165 John Denver Anthology –	02500987 John Mayer – Continuum $16.95	Live in Concert 2006 . . . .$19.95
Revised $22.95	02500681 John Mayer – Heavier Things . . .$16.95	02500196 Barbra Streisand –
02500002 John Denver Christmas $14.95	02500563 John Mayer – Room for Squares$16.95	A Love Like Ours $16.95
02502166 John Denver's Greatest Hits $17.95	02500081 Natalie Merchant – Ophelia $14.95	02503617 John Tesh – Avalon $15.95
02502151 John Denver – A Legacy	02500863 Jason Mraz – Mr. A-Z $17.95	02502178 The John Tesh Collection $17.95
in Song (Softcover) $24.95	02501467 Jason Mraz – We Sing.	02503623 John Tesh – A Family Christmas $15.95
02502152 John Denver – A Legacy	We Dance. We Steal Things. . . .$19.99	02503630 John Tesh – Grand Passion $16.95
in Song (Hardcover) $34.95	02502895 Nine $17.95	02500307 John Tesh – Pure Movies 2 . . . .$16.95
02500566 Poems, Prayers and Promises: The Art	02500425 Time and Love: The Art and	02501068 The Evolution of Robin Thicke . .$19.95
and Soul of John Denver $19.95	Soul of Laura Nyro $21.95	02500565 Thoroughly Modern Millie $17.99
02500326 John Denver –	02502204 The Best of Metallica $17.95	02501399 Best of Toto $19.99
The Wildlife Concert $17.95	02501336 Amanda Palmer –	02500576 Toto – 5 of the Best $7.95
02500501 John Denver and the Muppets:	Who Killed Amanda Palmer? . .$17.99	02502175 Tower of Power –
A Christmas Together $9.95	02501004 Best of Gram Parsons $16.95	Silver Anniversary $17.95
02501186 The Dresden Dolls –	02501137 Tom Paxton –	02501403 Keith Urban – Defying Gravity . .$17.99
The Virginia Companion $39.95	Comedians & Angels $16.95	02501008 Keith Urban – Love, Pain
02509922 The Songs of Bob Dylan $29.95	02500010 Tom Paxton – The Honor	& The Whole Crazy Thing . . .$17.95
02500586 Linda Eder – Broadway My Way $14.95	of Your Company $17.95	02501141 Keith Urban – Greatest Hits $16.99
02500497 Linda Eder – Gold $14.95	02507962 Peter, Paul & Mary –	02502198 The "Weird Al" Yankovic
02500396 Linda Eder –	Holiday Concert $17.95	Anthology $17.95
Christmas Stays the Same $17.95	02500145 Pokemon 2.B.A. Master $12.95	02502217 Trisha Yearwood –
02500175 Linda Eder –	02500026 The Prince of Egypt $16.95	A Collection of Hits $16.95
It's No Secret Anymore $14.95	02500660 Best of Bonnie Raitt $17.95	02500334 Maury Yeston –
02502209 Linda Eder – It's Time $17.95	02502189 The Bonnie Raitt Collection $22.95	December Songs $17.95
02500630 Donald Fagen – 5 of the Best. . . .$7.95	02502088 Bonnie Raitt – Luck of the Draw $14.95	02502225 The Maury Yeston Songbook . . .$19.95
02500535 Erroll Garner Anthology $19.95	02507958 Bonnie Raitt – Nick of Time $14.95	
02500318 Gladiator $12.95	02502218 Kenny Rogers – The Gift $16.95	
02502126 Best of Guns N' Roses $17.95	02500414 Shrek $16.99	
02502072 Guns N' Roses – Selections from	02500536 Spirit – Stallion of the Cimarron $16.95	
Use Your Illusion I and II $17.95	02500166 Steely Dan – Anthology $17.95	
02500014 Sir Roland Hanna Collection . . .$19.95	02500622 Steely Dan – Everything Must Go .$14.95	
02500856 Jack Johnson – Anthology $19.95	02500284 Steely Dan – Two Against Nature .$14.95	
02501140 Jack Johnson –	02500344 Billy Strayhorn:	
Sleep Through the Static $16.95	An American Master $17.95	
02500381 Lenny Kravitz – Greatest Hits . . .$14.95	02502132 Barbra Streisand –	
02501318 John Legend – Evolver $19.99	Back to Broadway $19.95	

See your local music dealer or contact:

0310